DOSTI

ਦੋਸਤੀ

لستی

STEEVEN TOOR SUKHNEER SIDHU

Kalam Creations Inc.
An Imprint of Kalam Creations Inc, Calgary AB

Visit us online at kalamcreations.ca

Printed in China
ISBN 978-1-7775485-2-0

The artwork for this book was created through hand drawings and composed digitally.

For my grandparents
-S.S

For my Nani ji
-S.T

FOREWORD

Prior to the partition of India and Pakistan, my family resided in the Bahawalpur State of Pakistan. My family was very well settled and had many acres of land that was primarily used for farming. Post-partition, many Sikhs continued to live in the Punjab region that fell within the Pakistan borders. Hindus and Sikhs that fled from Pakistan and Muslims that fled from India were forced to leave everything behind as they mass migrated across the newly drawn borders between the two nations. Prior to the partition, I had shifted to Allahabad, Punjab Pakistan where my uncle resided and was in the service there. I had a very close relationship with my uncle along with many of my family members, including my sister, who would regularly visit and stay with him. In 1947, the year partition took place, I was 13 years old.

Early in 1947, the conditions that loomed over us were still fairly stable. This was a time when the British were finally on the verge of leaving India. In March and April, small riots started to take place. Within a few months, the riots had spread quite rapidly across many regions of Punjab and other neighbouring states. As partition was declared in August of 1947, the violence had also peaked. It was beyond heartbreaking to witness the violence unfold right before our eyes and the atrocities we had to bear witness to. We had narrow escapes and many close calls as we attempted to reach safety in India. A Muslim officer helped my family tremendously, along with six other families, as he guided us to safety in India. The officer would stand watch over our vehicle when our families rested while reciting his daily prayers (Namaz). By avoiding major cities and roadways, it took us over 48 hours to reach the border and cross into India. It was truly a miracle that our families were able to safely make it across the border and reunite with our loved ones. My story is just one of many thousands that were impacted by the partition.

My message to the next generation is to truly believe in the principle of oneness and humanism; that we are all united as one human race. To rise above differences between one another and to have love for each other regardless of our faith or cultural differences. The need of the hour for today's generation is for peaceful coexistence. We might not have control over the house that we are born in, however, we do have the ability to love and support one another regardless of where we might come from.

Jaswant Singh Cheema

Special thanks to:

My Pakistani friends,
the Chaudhry family

Neha Jalali
Imreet Kaur
Guntas Kaur

A Long time ago...
In the land of FIVE RIVERS

Flows a story of
FRIENDSHIP..

Hurry up Chanh,
we are going to be LATE!

ਮੇਰੀ ਯਾਰੀ ਮੇਰੀ ਜ਼ਿੰਦਗੀ

میری یاری، میری زندگی ہے۔

"Meri Yaari Meri Zindgi"

"Oora Ooth"

Chanh and Manh
are headed home for the day
having some fun along the way

کل ملدے ہاں

ਕੱਲ ਮਿਲਦੇ ਹਾਂ

"See you tomorrow!"

Chanh, it's not safe for us here anymore
We need to Leave!

Chanh and his family left their home behind
to find safety in foreign lands

"I miss Manh"

"I miss Chanh"

"Meri Yaari"

& "Meri Zindgi"

To

Chanh became a musical star

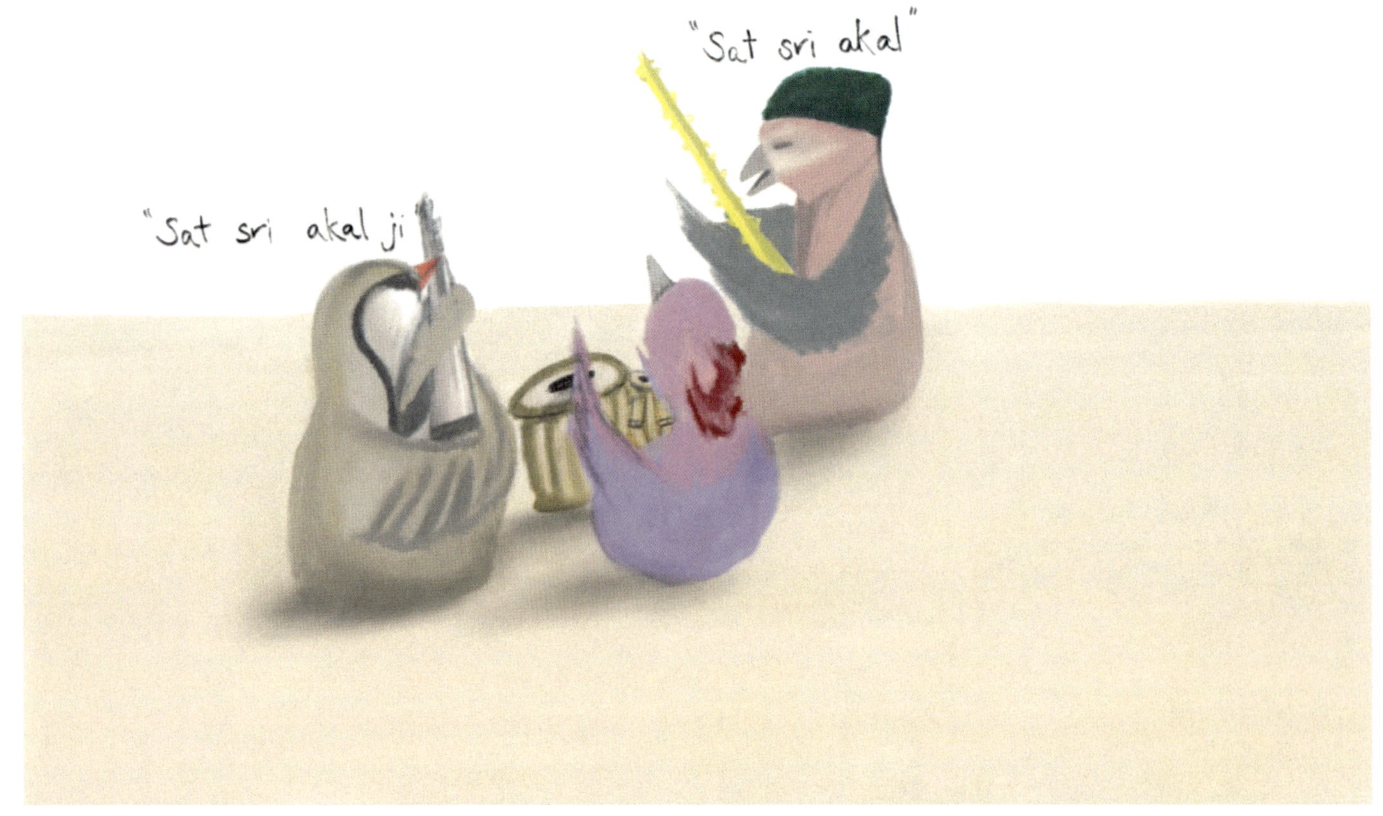

While Manh became an intelligent professor

moving to a new land far away

"Good Morning Class!"

"Wow, I really enjoyed this type of music growing up"

"Our first international tour!"

"How exciting!"

"This first song is dedicated to my childho

"Meri Yaari
Meri Zindgi"

od bestfriend Manh"

Tomorrow finally came...

آخر کار کل آگیا

ਆਖਿਰਕਾਰ ਕੱਲ ਆ ਗਿਆ

ABOUT THE CREATORS

Steeven Toor

was born in Abbotsford BC and raised in Calgary Alberta. He received his Bachelors from University of Calgary and Master of Public Health from Queen's University. Steeven strives to combine his background in public health with his creative talents as a writer and artist having worked on mental health advocacy through a creative lens in the South Asian community. Steeven has written and directed the award-winning documentary on Quebec's Bill 21 "Uproar" produced by Kalam creations and Revive Films.

Sukhneer Sidhu

was born and raised in Punjab before immigrating to Canada. She received her Bachelor of Science from University of Calgary and is currently a Master of Architecture candidate. Sukhneer has always been artistically curious and loves to be creative. Growing up, she remembers spending hours illustrating her own comic books. Her artwork addresses themes of identity and belonging and she strives to honor her roots through her work. This is her first picture book.

Made in the USA
Columbia, SC
12 October 2021

47077586R00022